LET'S PLAY!
LITTLE CHAMPS

BALLET

RYAN JAMES

NORWOOD HOUSE PRESS

Library of Congress Cataloging-in-Publication Data

Names: James, Ryan.
Title: Ballet / Ryan James.
Description: Buffalo, NY : Norwood House Press, 2025. | Series: Let's play! little champs | Includes glossary and index.
Identifiers: ISBN 9781684502356 (pbk.) | ISBN 9781684502363 (library bound) | ISBN 9781684502370 (ebook)
Subjects: LCSH: Ballet dancing--Juvenile literature. | Ballet--Juvenile literature.
Classification: LCC GV1787.5 J359 2025 | DDC 792.8--dc23

Published in 2025 by
Norwood House Press
2544 Clinton Street
Buffalo, NY 14224

Designer: Ocean Books
Editor: Kim Thompson

Photo credits: Cover, p. 1 VGstockstudio/Shutterstock.com; p 5 Waragic/Shutterstock.com; p. 6 Albina Sazheniuk/Shutterstock.com; pp. 7, 15 Maria Moroz/Shutterstock.com; pp. 11 chaponta/Shutterstock.com; p. 12 BearFotos/Shutterstock.com; p. 13 Lightfield Studios/Shutterstock.com; p. 14 Oksana Shuprych/Shutterstock.com; p. 17 Pavel L Photo and Video/Shutterstock.com; p. 18 Artur Didyk/Shutterstock.com; p. 19 Vytautas Kielaitis/Shutterstock.com; p. 21 Evheniy Pavlovski/Shutterstock.com

Printed in the United States of America

CPSIA compliance information: Batch #CW25NHP: For further information contact Norwood House Press at 1-800-237-9932.

TABLE OF CONTENTS

What Is Ballet?

Ballet is a type of dance. Ballet dancers move **gracefully**. They leap through the air. They perform to beautiful music. It takes lots of practice to dance smoothly and elegantly.

The Uniform

Ballet dancers wear **leotards**. They are tight and stretchy, so dancers can move easily. Thin, snug tights cover the dancer's legs.

Ballerinas wear fluffy skirts called tutus. Tutus have layers of light, floaty fabric.

Ballet slippers are soft and light. They are made from leather or canvas. Pointe shoes let dancers stay on the tips of their toes.

Ballet Class

Ballet dancers practice in a room called a **studio**. It has big mirrors, so dancers can watch themselves.

A ballet teacher shows the right way to move. The dancers **balance**, twirl, and leap.

Ballet Moves

For a plié, dancers lower their bodies as they bend their knees. They keep their backs straight and their heels on the floor.

For a pirouette, dancers spin on one foot. They pull the other foot up to the knee. They turn smoothly in circles.

For a jeté, dancers leap in the air. One leg stretches out in front and the other behind.

For an arabesque, dancers stand on one leg. The other leg lifts straight behind. The arms reach out to balance and to make a beautiful line.

Ballet Stories

Ballet dancers tell stories through dance. In *The Nutcracker*, Clara gets a **nutcracker** doll on Christmas. It comes to life and takes Clara on a magical adventure.

In *Swan Lake*, a **spell** turns the **princess** Odette into a swan. She meets a prince who tries to help her.

In *The Sleeping Beauty*, a spell puts the princess Aurora into a deep sleep. A prince breaks the spell with a kiss.

How to Be Performance-Ready

Ballet dancers should eat healthy foods like fruits, vegetables, and lean meats. They should drink plenty of water. Getting enough sleep gives them **energy** to perform at their best.

GLOSSARY

balance (BAL-uhns): to keep your body steady and upright

energy (EN-ur-jee): the ability to do work

gracefully (GRASE-ful-ee): with smoothness, ease, and beauty

leotards (LEE-uh-tahrdz): tight-fitting, one-piece garments worn for dancing, gymnastics, and exercise

nutcracker (NUHT-krak-ur): a tool with a lever that you pull down to crack a nut placed inside, often shaped and decorated to look like a soldier or other character

princess (PRIN-sehs): the daughter of a king or queen

spell (spel): words spoken to make magic happen; a magical curse

studio (STOO-dee-oh): a room or building in which an artist, dancer, or photographer works or practices

THINKING QUESTIONS

1. What do ballet dancers wear?
2. Why do you think ballet dancers wear slippers on their feet?
3. What is a pirouette?
4. Why do ballet dancers need to eat healthy foods?
5. What qualities do you think a good ballet dancer has?

INDEX

ABOUT THE AUTHOR

Ryan James lives in the western part of North Carolina with his rescue dog Bailey. As a child, he would search for creepy crawlies as he hiked through the forest near his house. When he's not on the hiking or biking trail, he is cheering on his favorite baseball and football teams.